THE BOUNTY

DEREK

WALCOTT

The Bounty

THE NOONDAY PRESS

FARRAR, STRAUS AND GIROUX

NEW YORK

The Noonday Press
A division of Farrar, Straus and Giroux
19 Union Square West, New York 10003

Copyright © 1997 by Derek Walcott
All rights reserved
Distributed in Canada by Douglas & McIntyre Ltd.
Printed in the United States of America
First published in 1997 by Farrar, Straus and Giroux
First Noonday edition, 1998

The Library of Congress has catalogued the hardcover edition as follows:
Walcott, Derek.
    The bounty / Derek Walcott. — 1st ed.
        p.   cm.
    ISBN 0-374-11556-7 (alk. paper)
        1. Saint Lucia—Poetry.   2. West Indies—Poetry.   I. Title.
    PR9272.9.W3B68   1997
    811—dc20   96-30546

Some sections of this book have appeared in The New Yorker.

Contents

ONE

THE BOUNTY

[*for Alix Walcott*]

i

Between the vision of the Tourist Board and the true
Paradise lies the desert where Isaiah's elations
force a rose from the sand. The thirty-third canto

cores the dawn clouds with concentric radiance,
the breadfruit opens its palms in praise of the bounty,
bois-pain, tree of bread, slave food, the bliss of John Clare,

torn, wandering Tom, stoat-stroker in his county
of reeds and stalk-crickets, fiddling the dank air,
lacing his boots with vines, steering glazed beetles

with the tenderest prods, knight of the cockchafer,
wrapped in the mists of shires, their snail-horned steeples
palms opening to the cupped pool—but his soul safer

than ours, though iron streams fetter his ankles.
Frost whitening his stubble, he stands in the ford
of a brook like the Baptist lifting his branches to bless

cathedrals and snails, the breaking of this new day,
and the shadows of the beach road near which my mother lies,
with the traffic of insects going to work anyway.

The lizard on the white wall fixed on the hieroglyph
of its stone shadow, the palms' rustling archery,
the souls and sails of circling gulls rhyme with:

"In la sua volontà è nostra pace,"
In His will is our peace. Peace in white harbours,
in marinas whose masts agree, in crescent melons

left all night in the fridge, in the Egyptian labours
of ants moving boulders of sugar, words in this sentence,
shadow and light, who live next door like neighbours,

and in sardines with pepper sauce. My mother lies
near the white beach stones, John Clare near the sea-almonds,
yet the bounty returns each daybreak, to my surprise,

to my surprise and betrayal, yes, both at once.
I am moved like you, mad Tom, by a line of ants;
I behold their industry and they are giants.

ii

There on the beach, in the desert, lies the dark well
where the rose of my life was lowered, near the shaken plants,
near a pool of fresh tears, tolled by the golden bell

of allamanda, thorns of the bougainvillea, and that is
their bounty! They shine with defiance from weed and flower,
even those that flourish elsewhere, vetch, ivy, clematis,

on whom the sun now rises with all its power,
not for the Tourist Board or for Dante Alighieri,
but because there is no other path for its wheel to take

except to make the ruts of the beach road an allegory
of this poem's career, of yours, that she died for the sake
of a crowning wreath of false laurel; so, John Clare, forgive me,

for this morning's sake, forgive me, coffee, and pardon me,
milk with two packets of artificial sugar,
as I watch these lines grow and the art of poetry harden me

into sorrow as measured as this, to draw the veiled figure
of Mamma entering the standard elegiac.
No, there is grief, there will always be, but it must not madden,

like Clare, who wept for a beetle's loss, for the weight
of the world in a bead of dew on clematis or vetch,
and the fire in these tinder-dry lines of this poem I hate

as much as I love her, poor rain-beaten wretch,
redeemer of mice, earl of the doomed protectorate
of cavalry under your cloak; come on now, enough!

iii

Bounty!
      In the bells of tree-frogs with their steady clamour
in the indigo dark before dawn, the fading morse
of fireflies and crickets, then light on the beetle's armour,

and the toad's too-late presages, nettles of remorse
that shall spring from her grave from the spade's heartbreak.
And yet not to have loved her enough is to love more,

if I confess it, and I confess it. The trickle of underground
springs, the babble of swollen gulches under drenched ferns,
loosening the grip of their roots, till their hairy clods

like unclenching fists swirl wherever the gulch turns
them, and the shuddering aftermath bends the rods
of wild cane. Bounty in the ant's waking fury,

in the snail's chapel stirring under wild yams,
praise in decay and process, awe in the ordinary
in wind that reads the lines of the breadfruit's palms

in the sun contained in a globe of the crystal dew,
bounty in the ants' continuing a line of raw flour,
mercy on the mongoose scuttling past my door,

in the light's parallelogram laid on the kitchen floor,
for Thine is the Kingdom, the Glory, and the Power,
the bells of Saint Clement's in the marigolds on the altar,

in the bougainvillea's thorns, in the imperial lilac
and the feathery palms that nodded at the entry
into Jerusalem, the weight of the world on the back

of an ass; dismounting, He left His cross there for sentry
and sneering centurion; then I believed in His Word,
in a widow's immaculate husband, in pews of brown wood,

when the cattle-bell of the chapel summoned our herd
into the varnished stalls, in whose rustling hymnals I heard
the fresh Jacobean springs, the murmur Clare heard

of bounty abiding, the clear language she taught us,
"as the hart panteth," at this, her keen ears pronged
while her three fawns nibbled the soul-freshening waters,

"as the hart panteth for the water-brooks" that belonged
to the language in which I mourn her now, or when
I showed her my first elegy, her husband's, and then her own.

But can she or can she not read this? Can you read this,
Mamma, or hear it? If I took the pulpit, lay-preacher
like tender Clare, like poor Tom, so that look, Miss!

the ants come to you like children, their beloved teacher
Alix, but unlike the silent recitation of the infants,
the choir that Clare and Tom heard in their rainy county,

we have no solace but utterance, hence this wild cry.
Snails move into harbour, the breadfruit plants on the *Bounty*
will be heaved aboard, and the white God is Captain Bligh.

Across white feathery grave-grass the shadow of the soul
passes, the canvas cracks open on the cross-trees of the *Bounty*,
and the Trades lift the shrouds of the resurrected sail.

All move in their passage to the same mother-country,
the dirt-clawing weasel, the blank owl or sunning seal.
Faith grows mutinous. The ribbed body with its cargo

stalls in its doldrums, the God-captain is cast adrift
by a mutinous Christian, in the wake of the turning *Argo*
plants bob in the ocean's furrows, their shoots dip and lift,

and the soul's Australia is like the New Testament
after the Old World, the code of an eye for an eye;
the horizon spins slowly and Authority's argument

diminishes in power, in the longboat with Captain Bligh.
This was one of your earliest lessons, how the Christ-Son
questions the Father, to settle on another island, haunted by Him,

by the speck of a raging deity on the ruled horizon,
diminishing in meaning and distance, growing more dim:
all these predictable passages that we first disobey

before we become what we challenged; but you never altered
your voice, either sighing or sewing, you would pray
to your husband aloud, pedalling the hymns we all heard

in the varnished pew: "There Is a Green Hill Far Away,"
"Jerusalem the Golden." Your melody faltered
but never your faith in the bounty which is His Word.

v

All of these waves crepitate from the culture of Ovid,
its sibilants and consonants; a universal metre
piles up these signatures like inscriptions of seaweed

that dry in the pungent sun, lines ruled by mitre
and laurel, or spray swiftly garlanding the forehead
of an outcrop (and I hope this settles the matter

of presences). No soul was ever invented,
yet every presence is transparent; if I met her
(in her nightdress ankling barefoot, crooning to the shallows),

should I call her shadow that of a pattern invented
by Graeco-Roman design, columns of shadows
cast by the Forum, Augustan perspectives—

poplars, casuarina-colonnades, the in-and-out light of almonds
made from original Latin, no leaf but the olive's?
Questions of pitch. Faced with seraphic radiance

(don't interrupt!), mortals rub their skeptical eyes
that hell is a beach-fire at night where embers dance,
with temporal fireflies like thoughts of Paradise;

but there are inexplicable instincts that keep recurring
not from hope or fear only, that are real as stones,
the faces of the dead we wait for as ants are transferring

their cities, though we no longer believe in the shining ones.
I half-expect to see you no longer, then more than half,
almost never, or never then—there I have said it—

but felt something less than final at the edge of your grave,
some other something somewhere, equally dreaded,
since the fear of the infinite is the same as death,

unendurable brightness, the substantial dreading
its own substance, dissolving to gases and vapours,
like our dread of distance; we need a horizon,

a dividing line that turns the stars into neighbours
though infinity separates them, we can think of only one sun:
all I am saying is that the dread of death is in the faces

we love, the dread of our dying, or theirs;
therefore we see in the glint of immeasurable spaces
not stars or falling embers, not meteors, but tears.

vi

The mango trees serenely rust when they are in flower,
nobody knows the name for that voluble cedar
whose bell-flowers fall, the pomme-arac purples its floor.

The blue hills in late afternoon always look sadder.
The country night waiting to come in outside the door;
the firefly keeps striking matches, and the hillside fumes

with a bluish signal of charcoal, then the smoke burns
into a larger question, one that forms and unforms,
then loses itself in a cloud, till the question returns.

Buckets clatter under pipes, villages begin at corners.
A man and his trotting dog come back from their garden.
The sea blazes beyond the rust roofs, dark is on us

before we know it. The earth smells of what's done,
small yards brighten, day dies and its mourners
begin, the first wreath of gnats; this was when we sat down

on bright verandahs watching the hills die. Nothing is trite
once the beloved have vanished; empty clothes in a row,
but perhaps our sadness tires them who cherished delight;

not only are they relieved of our customary sorrow,
they are without hunger, without any appetite,
but are part of earth's vegetal fury; their veins grow

with the wild mammy-apple, the open-handed breadfruit,
their heart in the open pomegranate, in the sliced avocado;
ground-doves pick from their palms; ants carry the freight

of their sweetness, their absence in all that we eat,
their savour that sweetens all of our multiple juices,
their faith that we break and chew in a wedge of cassava,

and here at first is the astonishment: that earth rejoices
in the middle of our agony, earth that will have her
for good: wind shines white stones and the shallows' voices.

vii

In spring, after the bear's self-burial, the stuttering
crocuses open and choir, glaciers shelve and thaw,
frozen ponds crack into maps, green lances spring

from the melting fields, flags of rooks rise and tatter
the pierced light, the crumbling quiet avalanches
of an unsteady sky; the vole uncoils and the otter

worries his sleek head through the verge's branches;
crannies, culverts, and creeks roar with wrist-numbing water.
Deer vault invisible hurdles and sniff the sharp air,

squirrels spring up like questions, berries easily redden,
edges delight in their own shapes (whoever their shaper).
But here there is one season, our viridian Eden

is that of the primal garden that engendered decay,
from the seed of a beetle's shard or a dead hare
white and forgotten as winter with spring on its way.

There is no change now, no cycles of spring, autumn, winter,
nor an island's perpetual summer; she took time with her;
no climate, no calendar except for this bountiful day.

As poor Tom fed his last crust to trembling birds,
as by reeds and cold pools John Clare blest these thin musicians,
let the ants teach me again with the long lines of words,

my business and duty, the lesson you taught your sons,
to write of the light's bounty on familiar things
that stand on the verge of translating themselves into news:

the crab, the frigate that floats on cruciform wings,
and that nailed and thorn-riddled tree that opens its pews
to the blackbird that hasn't forgotten her because it sings.

TWO

I cannot remember the name of that seacoast city,
but it trembled with summer crowds, flags, and the fair
with the terraces full and very French, determinedly witty,
as perhaps all Europe sat out in the open air
that was speckled and sun-stroked like Monet that summer
with its grey wide beach, ah yes! it is near Dinard,
a town with hyphens, I believe in Normandy
or Brittany, and the tide went far out and the barred
sand was immense. I was inhabiting a postcard.
The breeze was cold, but I did a good watercolour,
and it stands there on the wall. And though it is dated,
time races across its surface but nothing changes
its motion, the tidal flats not clouded, the tiny
figures in the distance, the man walking his dog. Any
stroke and tint have eluded time. Still, it estranges.
Now, so many deaths, nothing short of a massacre
from the wild scythe blindly flailing friends, flowers, and grass,
as the seaside city of graves expands its acre
and the only art left is the preparation of grace.
So, for my *Hic Jacet*, my own epitaph, "Here lies
D.W. This place is good to die in." It really was.

2 / SIGNS

[*for Adam Zagajewski*]

i

Europe fulfilled its silhouette in the nineteenth century
with steaming train-stations, gas-lamps, encyclopedias,
the expanding waists of empires, an appetite for inventory
in the novel as a market roaring with ideas.
Bound volumes echoed city-blocks of paragraphs
with ornate parenthetical doorways, crowds on one margin
waiting to cross to the other page; as pigeons gurgle epigraphs
for the next chapter, in which old cobbles begin
the labyrinth of a twisted plot; quiet heresies
over anarchic coffee in steaming cafés (too cold outdoors).
Opposite the closed doors of the Opera two green bronze horses
guard a locked square like bookends, while odours
of the decaying century drift over the gardens
with the smell of books chained in the National Library.
Cross a small bridge into our time under the pardons
of minor medieval saints and the light grows ordinary.
Look back down a linden boulevard that hazes
into a green mist that muffles its clopping horses,
its silk-hats, carriages, the moral width that was, say, Balzac's;
then return to this century of gutted, ashen houses
to the smoke that plumes from distant chimney stacks.

ii

Far from streets seething like novels with the century's sorrow
from charcoal sketches by Kollwitz, the émigré's pain
is feeling his language translated, the synthetic aura
of an alien syntax, an altered construction that will drain
the specific of detail, of damp: creaks of sunlight
on a window-ledge, under a barn door in the hay country
of boyhood, the linen of cafés in an academic light—
in short, the fiction of Europe that turns into theatre.
In this dry place without ruins, there is only an echo
of what you have read. It is only much later
that print became real: canals, churches, willows, filthy snow.
This is the envy we finally commit; this happens
to us readers, distant devourers, that its pages whiten
our minds like pavements, or fields where a pen's
track furrows a ditch. We become one of those, then,
who convert the scarves of cirrus at dusk to a diva's
adieu from an opera balcony, ceilings of cherubs, cornucopias
disgorging stone fruit, the setting for a believer's
conviction in healing music: then huge clouds pass,
enormous cumuli rumble like trucks with barrels of news-
print and the faith of redemptive art begins to leave us
as we turn back old engravings to the etched views
that are streaked with soot in wet cobbles and eaves.

iii

The cobbles huddle like shorn heads, gables are leaning
over a street to whisper, the walls are scraped of signs
condemning David's star. Grey faces are screening
themselves (like the moon drawing thin curtains
to the tramp of jackboots, as shattered glass rains
diamonds on the pavement). A remorseless silence
took the old tenants away; now there are signs
the streets dare not pronounce, far more their meaning,
why they occurred, but today the repetitions;
the fog clouding the cobbles, the ethnic cleaning.
Arc-lamps come on, and with them, the movie-setting,
the swastika shadows, and the gas-lamps punctuating
a street's interminable sentence. Linden leaves
blow past the closed Opera, and soot-eyed extras are waiting
for one line in a breadline. The shot elegiacally grieves
and the sequel moves with the orchestration of conscience
around the Expressionist corners of the Old Town.
Over accurate paraphernalia, the repeated signs
of a sequel, the cantor's echo, until the ancient tongue
that forbade graven images makes indifferent sense.

iv

That cloud was Europe, dissolving past the thorn branches
of the lignum-vitae, the tree of life. A thunderhead remains
over these islands in crests of arrested avalanches,
a blizzard on a screen in snow-speckled campaigns,
the same old news just changing its borders and policies,
beyond which wolves founder, with red berries for eyes,
and their unheard howling trails off in wisps of smoke
like the frozen cloud over bridges. The barge of Poland
is slowly floating downstream with magisterial
scansion, St. Petersburg's minarets a cloud. Then clouds
are forgotten like battles. Like snow in spring. Like evil.
All that seems marmoreal is only a veil.
Play Timon then, and curse all endeavour as vile,
let the combers continue to crest, to no avail.
Your shadow stays with you, startling the quick crabs
that stiffen until you pass. That cloud means spring
to the Babylonian willows of Amsterdam budding again
like crowds in Pissarro along a wet boulevard's branches,
and the drizzle that sweeps its small wires enshrouds
Notre Dame. In the distance the word Cracow
sounds like artillery. Tanks and snow. Crowds.
Walls riddled with bullet-holes that, like cotton-wool, close.

Then, as if the earth's wick were being lowered,
the glass of the grey sky was smudged and its field smoke trimmed,
October flared in New Hampshire while its leaves were laid
low by the whistling scythe as the sumac dimmed.
Then you heard the rasping screech of a wheeling falcon
over the silken asphalt road, past the burning lake
with its stilled reflecting timber, over burnt sheaves of tall corn
shriven and bearded in chorus, then a flake drifting
like the hawk's feather, to the earth's alarm: "It's snowing."
That flair for theatre, that motley, that harlequinade;
what else but a concert for our benefit, our going,
that processional flourish, a calendar's ambuscade,
with inns that sharply whiten, corn nailed to their door,
the pumpkin's *memento-mori*, the jack-o'-lantern's grin,
the sharp blue smell of smoke, the enriching odour
of decay, of consecration, in barns stocked with grain.
The flakes of November will carry you further into
a soundless country and the dark gather around
the lanterns of leaves, their piles of ash, then winter;
where you stand like an exclamation on a page of white ground.

Thanksgiving

Miraculous as when a small cloud of cabbage-whites
circles a bush, the first flakes of the season
spun over Brookline, on Beacon; the afternoon lights
would come on by four, but everyone said, "So soon?"
at the multiplying butterflies, though it was late November,
but also because they had forgotten the miracle,
though the trees were stricken and brief day's ember
didn't catch in their firewood; they did not recall
the elation of flakes and butterflies that their element
is a joy quickly forgotten, and thus with the fall
certainly gone, the leaves dimmed, their flare spent,
the old metaphor whispered to everyone's mouth
about age, white hair, the Arctic virginity of death,
that the flakes spun like ashes; but before my heart fled south,
my farewell confirmed by the signature of your breath,
white butterflies circling, settling in your hair, that could soothe
your closed eyelids trembling like cabbage-whites
on my island road, the sea's scales stuttering in the sun.

i / Christmas Eve

Can you genuinely claim these, and do they reclaim you
from your possible margin of disdain, of occasional escape:
the dusk in the orange yards of the shacks, the waxen blue-
green of the breadfruit leaves, the first bulb in the kitchens—shape
and shadow so familiar, so worn, like the handles of brooms
in old women's hands? The small river, the crammed shop
and the men outside it, and the stars that nail down their day.
In short, this affection for what is simple and known,
the direct faces, the deprived but resigned ones
whom you have exalted: are they utterly your own
as surely as your shadow is a thing of the sun's?
The sound rushing past the car windows, not the sea but cane,
the night wind in your eyes like a woman's hair, the fresh
fragrances, then the lights on the hills over Port of Spain,
the nocturnal intimacies that stroke the flesh.
Again, the night grows its velvet, the frogs croak
behind fences, the dogs bark at ghosts, and certainties
settle in the sky, the stars that are no longer questions.
Yes, they reclaim you in a way you need not understand:
candles that never gutter and go out in the breeze,
or tears that glint on night's face for every island.

ii

Days change, the sunlight goes, then it returns, and wearily,
under intense mental pain, I remember a corner
of brilliant Saddle Road climbing out of the valley
of leaf-quiet Santa Cruz, a passage with a bridge, one the
desperate memory fastens on even as it passes all the
other possible places; why this particular one?
Perhaps because it disembodies, it neutralises distance
with the shadows of leaves on the road and the bridge in the sun,
proving that it will remain in any of two directions,
leaving life and approaching the calm of extinction
with the blissful indifference with which a small stream
runs alongside the bridge and the flecked hills of Paramín
and the certainties (they were often of goodness)
that outweigh our coarse needs and the continuous amen
of the brown-shallowed river. Because memory is less
than the place which it cherishes, frames itself from nowhere
except to say that even with the shit and the stress
of what we do to each other, the running stream's bliss
contradicts the self-importance of despair
by these glittering simplicities, water, leaves, and air,
that elate dissolution which goes beyond happiness.

iii

Remember childhood? Remember a faraway rain?
Yesterday I wrote a letter and tore it up. Clouds carried bits under
    the hills
like gulls through the steam of the valley to Port of Spain;
then my eyes began to brim from all the old ills
as I lay face-up in bed, muffling the thunder
of a clouded heart while the hills dissolved in ruin.
This is how the rain descends into Santa Cruz,
with wet cheeks, with the hills holding on to snatches of sunlight
until they fade, then the far sound of a river, and surging grass,
the mountains loaded as the clouds that have one bright
fissure that closes into smoke, and things returning to fable
and rumour and the way it was once, it was like this once . . .
Remember the small red berries shaped like a bell
by the road bushes, and a church at the end of innocence,
and the sound of *la rivière Dorée*, through the trees to Choiseul,
the scent of hog plums that I have never smelled since,
the long-shadowed emptiness of small roads, when a singed smell
    rose
from the drizzling asphalt, the way rain hazes the chapel
of La Divina Pastora, and a life of incredible errors?

It depends on how you look at the cream church on the cliff
with its rusted roof and a stunted bell tower in the garden
off the road edged with white hard lilies. It could seem sad if
you were from another country, and your doubt did not harden
into pity for the priest in boots and muddy clothes who comes
from a county in Ireland you can't remember, where you felt
perhaps the same sadness for a stone chapel and low walls
heavy with time, an iron sea, and the history of the Celt
told as a savagery of bagpipes and drums.
Turn into this Catholic station, a peaked, brown vestry
and a bleating lamb in the grass. So the visitor believes
the wounded trunk in the shade of large almond leaves.
On a Saturday, shut, and a temperate sky, Blanchisseuse
closed and an elsewhere-remembering sea,
you too could succumb to a helpless shrug that says,
"God! the sad magic that is the hope of black people.
All their drumming and dancing, the ceremonies, the chants.
The *chantwell* screeching like a brass cock on a steeple.
The intricate, unlit labyrinth of their ignorance."
But I feel the love in his veined, mottled hands,
his lilt that lengthens "the road" and makes it Ireland's.

It is low tide, so the reef evolves into islands,
the ebb of History gives them distinction in turn,
the tide brings the stale reek of weed off the margins
of the old town, where thin banners of smoke would burn
from a midden near the canoes and that morose samaan
in whose shade fishermen squatted; the rusted enamel tin
of the moon stuck in the silt at the depth of the ochre river
and the choked canals were part of an imperial decay,
parliament and poor plumbing; plus whoever
chose irony over homesickness called it the Conway,
perhaps because it reflected the port of some county
with bright boats moored, rippled light, never mind the people;
in the nostalgia of an imperial sunset the name flared
over the shacks and limp nets and garbage until the flood
rose from its long ebb muttering Independence; they began to pull
down the banners that crumpled like smoke; they tore down
the shacks and bulldozed the midden, the long canoes slid
closer to the sea like caymans crouching; even the huge samaan
and its mossed branches surrendered its imperial shade
to where white offices rise. To look back like the sun
is to return to the reek of canals; the Conway is gone,
but from its shacks and their fishnets these lines were made.

i

My country heart, I am not home till Sesenne sings,
a voice with woodsmoke and ground-doves in it, that cracks
like clay on a road whose tints are the dry season's,
whose cuatros tighten my heartstrings. The shac-shacs
rattle like cicadas under the fur-leaved nettles
of childhood, an old fence at noon, *bel-air, quadrille,*
la comette, gracious turns, until delight settles.
A voice like rain on a hot road, a smell of cut grass,
its language as small as the cedar's and sweeter than any
wherever I have gone, that makes my right hand Ishmael,
my guide the star-fingered frangipani.
Our kings and our queens march to her floral reign,
wooden swords of the Rose and the Marguerite, their chorus
the lances of feathered reeds, ochre cliffs and soft combers,
and bright as drizzling banjos the coming rain
and the drizzle going back to Guinea, trailing her hem
like a country dancer. Shadows cross the plain
of Vieuxfort with her voice. Small grazing herds
of horses shine from a passing cloud; I see them
in broken sunlight, like singers remembering the words
of a dying language. I watch the bright wires follow
Sesenne's singing, sunlight in fading rain,
and the names of rivers whose bridges I used to know.

ii

The blades of the oleander were rattling like green knives,
the palms of the breadfruit shrugged, and a hissing ghost
recoiled in the casuarinas—they are as alien as olives—
the bougainvillea's lips divided, its mouth aghast;
it was on an ochre road I caught the noise of their lives,
how their rage was rooted, shaking with every gust:
their fitful disenchantment with all my turned leaves,
for all of the years while theirs turned to mulch, then dust.
"We offered you language early, an absolute choice;
you preferred the gutturals of low tide sucked by the shoal
on the grey strand of cities, the way Ireland offered Joyce
his own unwritten dirt road outside Choiseul."
"I have tried to serve both," I said, provoking a roar
from the leaves, shaking their heads, defying translation.
"And there's your betrayal," they said. I said I was sure
that all the trees of the world shared a common elation
of tongues, gommier with linden, *bois-campêche* with the elm.
"You lie, your right hand forgot its origin, O Jerusalem,
but kept its profitable cunning. We remain unuttered, undefined,"
and since road and sun were English words, both of them
endured in their silence the dividing wind.

iii

When the violin whines its question and the banjo answers,
my pain increases in stabs, my severances
from odours and roots, the homemade *shac-shac* scraping,
the dip and acknowledgement of courteous country dances,
the smoke I would hold in my arms always escaping
like my father's figure, and now my mother's; let me
for invocation's sacred sake, for the lonely hallowing
of leaves and turning corners, come on the breaking sea
around the sharp brown cliffs of Les Cayes, billowing
breaker, the salt Atlantic wind; I hear a language receding,
unwritten by you, and the voices of children reading
your work in one language only when you had both.
I should ask the clouds to stop moving, for the shadows
to pause, because I can feel it dying and the growth
of all that besieges it, the courtly gestures of grace.
My fingers are like thorns and my eyes are wet
like logwood leaves after a drizzle, the kind in which
the sun and the rain contend for the same place
like the two languages I know—one so rich
in its imperial intimacies, its echo of privilege,
the other like the orange words of a hillside in drought—
but my love of both wide as the Atlantic is large.

To recede like a snail flattening its enquiring horns
from nervous injuries, to fold like a moth's envelope
into the seam of the branches, to hurl keys over a cliff once
and for all, so that any exchange is as far as Europe,
is persecution's consequence. Howl, Timon, and turn
your scabbed back to the sun's fire, into the salt that seals it
with its stinging. The true faith is Job's poised curse
on a lost reputation, my name and the envy that steals it
and stuffs it between her thighs, and its mouldering purse.
The gnats sing of pollution in their ecstatic circles,
and antennae of a cockroach wriggle out of a washbasin,
and the termites, punctual as Harmattan, are like cycles
of locusts, and the sores are flowers and rosettes on my skin.
All I require is an acre of sunlight and salt wind. One acre
only, and nothing beyond that, with my own version
of the world beyond. I was here anyway, a maker
from boyhood. Watching how, after the rainy wind, the sea shone
like its fish, the scales danced, and my heart widened with the bay.
I should turn, like Timon, with every sneering wave,
from praise that might turn my head, and over my shoulder
give unembittered thanks for all a gift gave
as spray shatters against an indifferent boulder.

New creatures ease from earth, nostrils nibbling air,
squirrels abound and repeat themselves like questions,
worms keep enquiring till leaves repeat who they are,
but here we have merely a steadiness without seasons,
and no history, which is boredom interrupted by war.
Civilisation is impatience, a frenzy of termites
round the anthills of Babel, signalling antennae
and messages; but here the hermit crab cowers when it meets
a shadow and stops even that of the hermit.
A dark fear of my lengthened shadow, to that I admit,
for this crab to write "Europe" is to see that crouching child
by a dirty canal in Rimbaud, chimneys, and butterflies, old bridges
and the dark smudges of resignation around the coal eyes
of children who all look like Kafka. Treblinka and Auschwitz
passing downriver with the smoke of industrial barges
and the prose of a page from which I brush off the ashes,
the tumuli of the crab holes, the sand hourglass of ages
carried over this bay like the dust of the Harmattan
of our blown tribes dispersing over the islands,
and the moon rising in its search like Diogenes' lantern
over the headland's sphinx, for balance and justice.

The feel of the village in the afternoon heat, a torpor
that stuns chickens, that makes stones wish they could hide
from the sun at two, when to cross from door to door
is an expedition, when palm tree and almond hang their head
in dusty weariness, and drunk old women sit on broken canoes,
too tired to beg, and the young men have that dull stare
that says nothing, neither "Keep going" nor "Welcome." No noise
from the sea, the horizon dazzles; you are used to this,
but sometimes something else pierces and the shallows sigh it:
"Except for that enormous cloud that a frigate cruises,
ici pas ni un rien," they say, here there's nothing. *Nada*
is the street with its sharp shadows and the vendors quiet
as their yams, and strange to think the turrets of Granada
are *nada* compared to this white-hot emptiness, or all the white
stone castles in summer, or pigeons exploding into flocks
over St. Mark's, *nada* next to the stride-measuring egret,
compared to the leisurely patrolling of the frigate
over the stunned bay, and the crash of surf on the rocks.
It is only your imagination that finally ignites it
at sunset in that half-hour the colour of regret,
when the surf, older than your hand, writes: "It
is nothing, and it is this nothingness that makes it great."

There is nothing except the sun at the end of the street
and a hot sea framed between the decaying houses,
then a limp and listless wave rising from the heat
like an old man's hand brushing gnats from his eyes
and a file of canary-coloured ducklings. This is Gros-Ilet,
with a Sunday stretched out in its bed, to the sadness
of an ice-cream van whirring its mechanical tune
over and over, and all your sins spin in that noise,
your childhood, and now your grandchildren in turn,
like a shepherdess slowly turning on a music-box,
silvery and sparkling like a drizzle in the sun.
There is the glare of emptiness at three in the afternoon
where a dozing vendor watches the asphalt burn.
You might as well cross yourself and expect no pardon
for the things you continue to do and those that were done,
the way that the dead street does not expect a drizzle
hearing the dark dove coo and the blackbird whistle
in the thorn grove as a cool wind suddenly stirs
the bamboo plot and it threshes, in a cool change of air,
when every name that filled your head was "hers"
and now it is past the ecstasy of despair;
a blackbird drinks and shakes it off with two shudders
of its wings and vanishes across the wild garden.

The phrases of a patois rooted in this clay hillside
blow with the blossoms of the cedar; earth cracks as
if it were an old coal-pot, with handles, *morceaux-*
    chaudière,
and a dry music begins: cicada gourds of maracas,
the silver dazzle of banjos, violins scraping air,
how the cedar is silent sticks against the blue drought,
the last flare of a language turning in the blazing leaves
by the cobalt Atlantic that change will soon put out.
All that was shapely, the wood that the joiner believes,
the baker drawing loaves from the clay with his oar,
smell, shape, and sound going out of the earth's fragrance,
with the phrase "It was so. We don't speak so anymore,"
till a silence settles on language made with our hands.
The silence of white hotels, the frilled sleeves of a shore
that carries a menu translated in the speech of the islands
that waiters and receptionists disown. "Is not so anymore."
There is a tree I know that groans when it bends
accommodating the wind. At first, because of its heaving,
I thought the earth shook in the shade of thorned acacias,
but I had rested my sole on a trunk, and its grieving
came from its roots underground; if earth heaves like us
then the dead, even in their silence, may still be breathing.

Never get used to this; the feathery, swaying casuarinas,
the morning silent light on shafts of bright grass,
the growling *Aves* of the ocean, the white lances of the marinas,
the surf fingering its beads, hail heron and gull full of grace,
since that is all you need to do now at your age
and its coming serene extinction like the light on the shale
at sunset, and your gift fading out of this page;
your soul travelled the one horizon like a quiet snail,
infinity behind it, infinity ahead of it,
and all that it knew was this craft, all that it wanted—
what did it know of death? Only what you had read of it,
that it was like a flame blown out in a lowered lantern,
a night, but without these stars, the prickle of planets, lights
like a vast harbour, or devouring oblivion;
never get used to this, the great moon on these studded nights
that make the heart stagger; and the stirring lion
of the headland. This is why you have ended, to pass,
praising the feathery swaying of the casuarinas
and those shudderings of thanks that so often descended,
the evening light in the shafts of feathery grass,
the lances fading, then the lights of the marinas,
the yachts studying their reflections in black glass.

Great bursts of exaltation crest the white breaker,
deep-drawn as the sighing shale, as the heart's salt history,
as you stand like a pilgrim on the edge of this acre
of bleached grass and rocks under the frigate's glory,
with stalks that whistle to the scyther's massacre
of the forked frangipani, each flower a *memento-mori*.
The blue hills are fixed in waves on the Northern Range,
and I look out from Becune Point with deaths inside me,
and that nature is so pitiless in its beauty is still strange;
over there, against the indigo-blue Santa Cruz
mountains, the immortelle ignites its branches with orange
blossoms, however briefly, while the incredible blue is
as indifferent as ever. The clouds change governments,
and Ben is gone, and John, Godfrey, and Quentin; the news
is always of a fading, like the distant instruments
of a parang band on the breeze to the bright poui's
mute detonations. Look, they were not mine, but these
things I borrowed I bequeath you, my daughters, as you will
bequeath your own children every joy that was lent,
hoping the blossoms of these leaves were carefully spent,
to the *cuatros* of Christmas, the orange tree against the blue hill.

16 / SPAIN

i

Near our ochre pastures with real bulls, your clay one
braces the kitchen lintel. How earthen every noun sounds
with red tiles, bell-tower in level light--Rioja, Aragon!
It stands on its four-square shadow with crescent horns
alert for a shaken red leaf, for the rising sounds,
like the shoal, an inlet of intaken breath, then the roar
as it lowers and gallops on feather hooves hooking air
near the cockerel's strut of the spangled man turning away
from a mirror of sand with "Yes, but I am not ready."
The wave-roar of *olés* cresting from the arena
where the earth is cracked and the only things green are
the spiked agave on the cliff bringing the dust of Navarre
across the ocean. I was never warned about this,
that your flame-straight cypresses sway like our casuarinas,
that those who have seen Spain in the oven of August
are scorched in their hearts forever as herds of dust
drift with these bulls whose model is this small clay ghost.
Swallow of my memory, let us fly south to fierce spaces,
arrowing to Granada through monotonous olives,
towards faint blue mountains to a folk fierce and gracious,
along iron gorges whose springs glitter like knives.

ii / Granada

Red earth and raw, the olive clumps olive and silver
in the thud of wind like a cape shaping the car,
the tormented olives smaller than you thought they were,
as a sadness, not incalculable but measured,
its distance diminishing in the humming coil of the road
widens astonishing Granada. This is how to read
Spain, backwards, like memory, like Arabic, mountains
and predicted cypresses confirming that the only tense
is the past, where a sin lies that is all of Spain's.
It writhes in the olive's trunk, it gapes in the ochre
echo of a stone hillside, like a well's dry mouth: "Lorca."
The black olives of his eyes, the bread dipped in its saucer.
A man in a torn white shirt with its wine-stains,
a black suit, and leather soles stumbling on the stones.
You cannot stand outside, apart from it, and the other ones
on the open hill, the staccato of carbine-fire,
of the dancer's heels, the O of the flamenco singer
and the mouth of the guitar; they are there in Goya,
the clown that dies, eyes open, in *The Third of May*
where the heart of Spain is. Why Spain will always suffer.
Why do they return from this distance, this far away
from the cypresses, the mountains, the olives turning silver?

iii / Reading Machado

The barren frangipani branches uncurl their sweet threat
out of the blue. More echoes than blossoms, they stun the senses
like the nocturnal magnolia, white as the pages I read,
with the prose printed on the left bank of the page
and, on the right, the shale-like speckle of stanzas
and the seam, like a stream stitching its own language.
The Spanish genius bristling like thistles. What provoked this?
The pods of a dry season, heat rippling in cadenzas,
black ruffles and the arc of a white throat?
All echoes, all associations and inferences,
the tone of Antonio Machado, even in translation,
the verb in the earth, the nouns in the stones, the walls,
all inference, all echo, all association,
the blue distance of Spain from bougainvillea verandahs
when white flowers sprout from the branches of a bull's horns,
the white frangipani's flowers like the white souls of nuns.
Ponies that move under pines in the autumn mountains,
onions, and rope, the silvery bulbs of garlic, the creak
of saddles and fast water quarrelling over clear stones,
from our scorched roads in August rise these heat-cracked stanzas,
all inferences, all echoes, associations.

iv

Storks, ravens, cranes, what do these disparate auguries mean?
The sky ripened then dulled, then across the chimneys
the storks, their legs dangling as if broken, found their nests
over the arches of Alcalá, the cobbled city of Cervantes,
arches and punishing bells, on your wrist a thought rests
like a settling crow. Your death is closer than an ant, as
you look to the day ahead, bountiful, abundant.
I look up at the dry hill in the sun, each shadow a thought.
I imagine my absence; the fatigued leaves will
fall one by one into soundless brown grass in drought
and the raw ochre patches where lilac laces the hill
and the shadows returning exactly some May as they ought,
but with the seam of air I inhabited closed.
A gusting of orange petals crosses Santa Cruz
in a bridal breeze; here combers bouquet in white lace,
and I offer these lines with their thorns to whoever can use
them, the scales of my two islands swayed into place.
I bequeath my eyes to whoever admires Paramín,
my ears to the caves of Las Cuevas, when the silver knot is loosed
from nerve-strings and arteries, and cloud-pages close in amen.

Down shortcuts like wounds in the hills, into estate kitchens,
erect old women brought tributary provisions,
tubers crusted with dirt, Yoruba yams, rusted dasheens,
their clay-pipes oracular ovens, their eyes grey stones.
They diced roots in clay-pots; they were vessels themselves
    containing
the gods dying inside them, imprecations, medicines,
chants for the moon in full flight, and the full moon waning
into a sickle; they read earth's cracked palm for signs.
Queens of interior kingdoms from Bahia to Cuba,
they crouched, webbed in their shuddering séance
connected by ceremonies, by phrases of forgotten Yoruba,
I come to them as a dark king, but in self-defence,
frogs plucked and popped in my mind's cauldron, the hysteria
that gnaws under the stone of my skull riddling my sense
in the white nights I spent staring at the ceiling's terror.
Preservers of foetuses, since I have no wish to return
coiled like a shrimp to the amniotic basin,
nor to my roots, earth's womb, with my tubers torn
from simple multiplying necessity; if to keep sane
you must blast their derision with chancres, wither their envy,
then do it, benign ones, but I have no zeal to be Thane
of Cawdor, or an island's king. Only from autumn's fog let me
wake, cloaked by the sea-wind on my own coast again.

Not the horned head, the beaked visor, the threshing vans
veined like expanding umbrellas beating up from the sulphur,
fears from a hole in the brain, the bubbling ovens
where heads rise and sink in Omega and Alpha;
not the legion of bats at dusk with the screeches of children,
given even the porous moonscape with its mineral hues
of rust, fool's gold, leprous dermis and toothless sockets—
that is simply the geology of hell, what hell unbearably has
is the soft sound of fears beating on the brain's wall, pockets
of sucked-in vertigo, the slow confirmation of error
on waking into ordinary light, or spooning out coffee
and pausing for a second paralysed by the terror
of memory. The astonishment of self-contempt, the offer
of the breaking day to redeem the self, the dying
of faith in the monodic flute of the ground-dove
trying to connect with melody, trying and trying
in the dry grove up on the hill, how even now love
can still wound and can crawl into the mind's hole,
huddled there, starved and longing to die. No, above,
there are no armadas of locusts, no prince, no bright soul
pitching like a meteor, no tragic arc in its falling,
only a flute in the head, the note of a ground-dove calling.

What is this virulence that eats at the cloth of the altar,
riddling its foam like the sea's lace, the space between the holes
or the fibre that knits them, the sound of the turned Psalter
multiplied into beating wings? There is no simile for our souls
if they are winged but insubstantial, there is no sound
like coveys whirring from grass, elusive shoals
of mackerel from the brain's coral, shadows racing over sand.
Bright day, rippled morning, breakers and strokes of white sails,
widening wings of the frigate bird and the tilting gull,
at this very hour, in different islands, are they all one sound,
the mute hymn of glory, the groundswell of death, both
    beautiful?
Rest, Clara Rosa. They all share a common ground,
and no sea is heavier than my heart, which is full.
Back to earth, clear rose, close the wrinkled petals of your eyes!
The leaves sparkle, the grass is beaded, sorrow dries
from the concrete patches. Now they are taking you where
repetition and process continue, the sea, the blue days,
the fire of our flowers, the seraphic, the infinite air.
Which your red mouth is part of now, with its loud, easy laughter.

The bamboo stands ready as an army with its plumed banners;
the mountains blacken and you feel afraid for the flowers;
a heraldic heron moves under the wild bananas;
both the weather in the house and the weather outside the house
are the same, cannon-fire clouds, the reeds by the river's drain
bend in a wind that is steadying, multiplying the ripples
near the stones; now wind threshes the tall cane,
like the charging sea or a theatre's distant applause.
Distant and dying applause, the dark mountain of Santa Cruz,
and the chapel in the play, the curtains of all the plays
drawn over the bright grass, like clouds, the gift you use
to examine this sadness moves as wide as the ocean,
an amnesiac cloud crossing the Caroni Plain
like the Ganges, the flags and small creeks, and your devotion
to pursue those bleached tracks that disappear into bush, in the
　　　rain—
something of weight in the long indigo afternoon,
the yam vines trying to hide the sugar-wheel's ruin;
something unconnected, oblique as if, after the motion
of history, every object we named was not the correct noun.

i

This is the first fiction: the biblical plague of dragonflies
crossing the plumes of bamboo after the huge rains
that we thought were locusts, they were there; what magnifies
their importance is plot, to believe that the fiction begins
with the lift of astonishing insects from the very first line.
Horses stamp at the lassoes of gnats, and the sweet odour
of their dung mixes with the smell of grass drying,
and I watch the mountains steaming from the sunlit door.
There is symmetry in all this, or all fiction is lying.
Pray for a life without plot, a day without narrative,
but the dragonflies drift like a hive of adjectives loosened
from a dictionary, like bees from the hive of the brain,
and as time passes, they pass, their number is lessened
and their meaning no more than that they come after rain.
They come after rain to this valley when the bamboos have calmed
themselves after threshing and plunging like the manes of horses,
they come with the pestilential host of a prophet armed
for the day of the locust. What summoned their force is
nowhere to be seen, yet the frightening hum of their wings
cruising the garden carries echoes of ancient affliction,
revisitants who have come to remind us of our first wrongs,
grenade-eyed and dragonish; neither science nor fiction.

ii

He believed the pain of exile would have passed
by now, but he had stopped counting the days and months,
and lately the seasons, given the promise that nothing can last
for a whole life, much less forever, that if we have suffered once,
but thoroughly, a particular loss, we would not suffer it again
in the same way, so that what he counted were the years
whose number he did not repeat aloud, but he knew if rain
fell and after rain the wind swept the plazas, his tears
dried as quickly as the fading sheets of concrete
facing the national park and its bicycle paths
and the drizzle-like silver of wheels, that the heat
of summer in one of the kindest cities of Europe was
nothing compared to the inferno of August at home.
He mutters to himself in the old colonial diction
and he heard how he still said home not only to appease
his hope that he would be there soon, but that he would come
to the rail of the liner and see the serrated indigo ridges
that had waited for him, and all the familiar iron
roofs, and even the vultures balancing on the hot ledges
of the Customs House. He wears black, his hair has grown
white, and he has placed his cane on a bench in the park.
There is no such person. I myself am a fiction,
remembering the hills of the island as it gets dark.

iii

He carried his tenebrous thoughts in and out of shadows
like a leopard changing its covert, to find a speckled quiet
appropriate to contemplation, as its yellow eyes close
on a needling yawn, replete with nothing, with emptiness, yet
loaded with its pumping, measured peace, like a herd of zebras
carrying the striped shade of grasses to a watering hole
but in the steadiness of heads and hooves, their fetlocks brace
for a sudden sidewise clatter. The leaves and shadows heal;
all lie down benignly in the thorn-trees' satisfaction,
lion and jackal, when noon is the peaceable kingdom;
they stretch, shudder, and are still, the only action
in their slowly swivelling eyes. Here under the fierce dome
of a cloudless August he feels how the languor that climbs
from stomach to slow-lidding eyes and leonine yawn
shudders in his haunches and crawls along his limbs,
a peace that goes as far back as the umbrella thorn-trees
into a quiet close to Eden, before a dark thought like a cloud
raced over the open grass, and his trotting stalker, lioness,
crouched and, shifting her poise, pounced! Then a small crowd
of hopping, opening vultures and the speckled hyenas.

iv

He endured a purgatorial November, but one
without fire, whose smoke was only the loaded mist
that steamed through the charred woods, where a round sun
peered dimly as it travelled and where shadows were amazed
at any brightness on sidewalk and on ochre wall,
but which the law of seasons faded and slowly erased
as an error. He moved through its crowds like a criminal,
summoning what grace he could find in the lightest
gesture, the casual phrase, holding a cup, eating
without hanging his head, and on those, the brightest
hours that sometimes lanced the grey light, repeating
to himself that this was not his climate or people, no season
as depleting as this, and beyond this there was the sea
and the unrelenting mercy of light, a window in the prison
his mind had become; that suffering was easy
if, beyond it, there was the truth of another sky
and different trees that fitted his nature, his hand
that for ail of its sixty-five years had tried not to lie
any more than a crab could travelling its page of sand.
The days would darken with cold, more leaves would die
behind fences, the fog thicken, but beyond them was the good
    island.

v

He could hear the dogs in the distance, and their baying
led him towards the chapel that rose off the road,
but he did not enter it. This was beneath praying,
and the black dogs were only his thoughts from nights of dread
through the rigid and guerdoning forests of Santa Cruz;
his heart hobbles, bubbling blood like berries on its trail,
three or four palms crest there, and the crazed parrot-cries
are like the clatter of testimony from an obscene trial,
but they cross the rose sky and fade, and a solace returns.
In the hot, hollow afternoon a shout crosses the valley,
a hawk glides, and behind the flame of the immortelle a hill burns
with a flute of blue smoke; this is all there is of value.
O leaves, multiply the days of my absence and subtract them
from the humiliation of punishment, the ambush of disgrace
for what they are: excrement not worthy of any theme,
not the burl and stance of a cedar or the pliant grass,
only the scorn of indifference, of weathering out abuse
like the lissome plunge of branches tossing with the grace
of endurance, bowing under the way that bamboo obeys
the horizontal gusts of the rain, not as martyrdom
but as natural compliance; below him was a house
where without a wound he was more than welcome,
and kind dogs came to the gate jostling for his voice.

vi / Manet in Martinique

The teak plant was as stiff as rubber near the iron railing
of the pink verandah at whose centre was an arch
that entered a tenebrous, overstuffed salon with the usual sailing
ship in full course through wooden waves, shrouds stiff with starch,
and around, in dolefully tinted cosmetic photos,
a French family: bearded grandpapa and black-bunned *grand-
    mère*
pillows with tassels, porcelains, souvenirs like prose
that had lost its bouquet, Lafcadio Hearn, the usual Flaubert,
more travel memoirs, a Japanese vase, one white rose
of immortal wax. My host left to make a phone-call.
I felt an immeasurable sadness for the ship's sails,
for the stagnant silence of objects, the mute past they carry,
for the glimpse of Fort-de-France harbour through lattices,
"Notre âme est un trois-mâts cherchant son Icarie"—
Baudelaire on the wandering soul. This was in the false métropole
of Martinique. A fan stirred one of Maupassant's tales.
Where was the spirit of the house? Some cliché with kohl-
lined eyes, lips like Manet's bougainvillea petals.
I sensed the salon, windows closed, was trying to recall
all it could of Paris; I turned from the wall, and there,
hollow with longing as the wall's gilt-framed clipper,
near stiff rubber leaves in the charged afternoon air,
unsheathed from her marble foot, a red satin slipper.

I am considering a syntax the colour of slate,
with glints of quartz for occasional perceptions and
winking mica for wit. I am not weary of the elate,
but grey days are useful, without reflection, like the drained sand
just after twilight. I am considering the avoidance of
an excitable vocabulary or a melodramatic pause like death,
or the remorse of loss or not; there is no loss without love,
but this too must be muted, like the metronome of breath
close to the even heart. Pause. Resume. Pause. Once more.
A grey horse, riderless, grazes where the grass is gone,
a slate-coloured horse wrenching tufts on a cold shore,
and the last lurid gash going, the sun closing its house
for the night, and everything near extinction. Even remorse.
Especially remorse and regret and longing and noise,
except the waves in the dark that strangely console
with their steadiness. They are bringing the same old news,
not only the death-rattle of surf on the gargling shoal,
but something further than the last wave, the smell
of pungent weed, of dead crabs whose casings whiten,
and further than the stars that have always looked too small
for those infinite spaces (Pascal) that used to frighten.
I am considering a world without stars and opposites. When?

I saw stones that shone with stoniness, I saw thorns
steady in their inimical patience. Now I see nothing after
the lizard has scuttled; I create each response
when there is no balance, neither tears nor laughter
nor life nor death, nor the sequence of tenses;
that is, I can see no past and foresee no future,
for the stones shine in their stoniness, and the logwood thorns
are waiting for nothing, not to be plaited into a crown,
or the lizard to throb on the side of the road as the frog would
till I passed. I see this also as beyond declension,
and not a commemoration of the invincible is
that changes itself as it proceeds, the past's extension,
or the afternoon-long shadows that are the future's.
Therefore, I foresee myself as blessedly invisible,
anonymous and transparent as the wind, a leaf-light traveller
between branches and stones, the clear, the unsayable
voice that moves over the uncut grass and the yellow
bell of an allamanda by the wall. All of this will soon
be true, but without sorrow, the way stones allow
everything to happen, the way the sea shines in the sun,
silver and bountiful in the slow afternoon.

Alphaeus Prince. What a name! He was one of the Princes.
He died, a boy, as so many princes did in literature,
in English history, of a fierce obscure disease,
a regal and privileged fever; we envied him the Tower,
the ermine and mink and the orb; he so simply entered
legend, which death was to us children suffering
that radiated glory that withheld its own crown
until Alphaeus Prince one day would be Alphaeus King,
which was not ordained by fate, so that the promise and prize
of his name would always float over each bowed head
as we imagined his smooth brown skin, his large black eyes
closed in the superior knowledge of being dead.
Brighter than me, but darker (that mattered then
and still does, not here so much, but the world beyond).
What was his future in a world that was ruled by men
Milton and Cromwell's colour? Princes and angels were blond.
Fifty years later, why should the name spring
into mind, or aim like a shaft of light in the mind
further back than the friends I know who have been dying
as if from some medieval plague. This morning the sea-wind
is fresh, the island shines in light, and I think of a boy
I loved for his beauty, his wit, his eyes, which to me carried
a glint of their brevity, whose name still carries joy
in it, and who made death a gift that we quietly envied.

These lines that I write now, that lack salt and motion,
these branches that lack colour, astonishment, smell,
are not less than the aisles of the waves in their devotion,
or the heart-startling explosions of the immortelle.
Width, and light. The mildly pronounced benediction
of trees saying their beads, the bamboos bent over their pews,
their sacrament flares again, from the dawn's ignition
of orange flames in the great pouis of Santa Cruz,
the cold road past the closed chapel, the cocoa-groves there
still dark, the hills start to lighten their ridges
and, to exhaust the metaphor in the way that too much prayer
exhausts us, the murmurous responses of midges
drone their litany, echoing in the chancel of the head
as you walk in the glorious morning of the dry season
reciting the names on the stones of the increasing dead,
who are past questioning now, past the cracked heart, past reason,
and even bewilderment as the upper region
of the sky is a ceiling of wan orange and saffron
cumuli and indigo cirrus, and that seraphic legion
crosses north to more waking islands, after the suffering
that comes in the dead hours before dawn. Open the door.
The winged moon is pinned to its curtain like a night moth,
and the heart kneels to the sea-light. Its task? To adore
at the wide and chafing foam-fringed altar-cloth.

The sublime always begins with the chord "And then I saw,"
following which apocalyptic cumuli curl and divide
and the light with its silently widening voice might say:
"From that whirling rose that broadens its rings in the void
here come my horsemen: Famine, Plague, Death, and War."
Then the clouds are an avalanche of skulls torrentially rolling
over a still, leaden sea. And here beginneth the season
when the storm-birds panic differently and a bell starts tolling
in the mind from the rocking sea-wash (there is no such sound),
but that is the sway of things, which has the necks of the coconuts
bending like grazing giraffes. I stood on the dark sand
and then I saw that darkness which I gradually accepted
grow startling in its joy, its promised anonymity
in its galloping breakers, in time and the space that kept it
immortal and changing without the least thought of me,
the serrated turret of a rock and the white horse that leapt it,
that spumed and vaulted with the elation of its horsemen,
a swallowing of a turmoil of a vertiginous chaos,
the delight of a leaf in a sudden gust of force when
between grey channels the islands are slowly erased
and one dare not ask of the thunder what is its cause.
Let it be written: The dark days also I have praised.

Praise to the rain, eraser of picnics, praise the grey cloud
that makes every headland a ghost, and the guttering belch-
braided water, praise to the rain and her slow shroud,
she is the muse of Amnesia which is another island,
spectral and adrift where those we still love exist
but in another sense, that this shore cannot understand,
for reminding us that all substance thins into mist
and has its vague frontiers, the country of memory
and, as in Rimbaud, the idea of eternity,
is a razed horizon when the sky and the sea are mixed
and the solid disappears like the dead into essences
which is the loud message of the martial advancing rain
with its lances and mass and—sometimes alarming our senses—
the kettledrums of advancing thunder. Before her the grain
bows and darkens, the tide cowers then rises, the air
becomes palpable and our nerves assemble for a siege
in the shut eyes and clamped doors of our body, her hair
horizontal in the wind blown back like the surge,
the casuarinas whine and sway in the wind, two drops
startle the flesh and the sun withdraws behind drapes
like a king or a president on the palace balcony
who hears the roar of a square and thinks it is only
the rain, it will pass, tomorrow will be sunny,
praise to the rain its hoarse voice dissolver of shapes,
of the peaks of power, princes, and mountain slopes.

Awaking to gratitude in this generous Eden,
far from frenzy and violence in the discretion of distance,
my debt, in Yeats's phrase, to "the bounty of Sweden"
that has built this house facing white combers that stands
for hot, rutted lanes far from the disease of power,
spreads like that copper-beech tree whose roots are Ireland's,
with a foam-haired man pacing around a square tower
muttering to a grey lake stirred by settling swans,
in the glare of reputation; whose declining hour
is exultation and fury both at once.
There is no wood whose branches bear gules of amber
that scream when they are broken, no balsam cure,
nothing beyond those waves I care to remember,
but a few friends gone, and that is a different care
in this headland without distinction, where December
is as green as May and the waves soothe in their unrest.
I heard the brass leaves of the roaring copper-beech,
saw the swans white as winter, names carved on the breast
of the tree trunk in the light and lilt of great speech,
and the prayer of a clock's hands at noon that come to rest
over Ireland's torment. No bounty is greater
than walking to the edge of the rocks where the headland's
detonations exult in their natural metre,
like white wings at Coole, the beat of his clapping swans.

If these were islands made from mythologies where
the thudding bow remembers the crescent it is headed for,
not merely a blinding cay with incredible water,
but there a wet, black-haired woman, and here a monster,
and, past them, more shoals and perils, candelabraed squid
above ululating coves, would deeper attention be paid
to the shallows' scriptures, and what the headland hid,
would the Y's and W's of circling frigates be read
from an augur's old alphabet, the secrets their entrails hid?
When a keel grates the sand and a sandpiper scuttles
backwards, what is memory, and what action is our own?
What patterned then unravelled threads does the surf return,
other than the wanderer's shadow on scorching stone,
if all the other mythologies were forcefully forgotten,
the bronze-hammerer, the wind-weaver, Hephaestus for Ogun?
That rusted bucket is not a funerary urn.
Yet those silver currents threaded the old tapestries
with dolphins and dragons, and embroidering seams
followed channels winding from the Pillars of Hercules
to this width. In maps the Caribbean dreams
of the Aegean, and the Aegean of reversible seas.

[*for Sigrid*]

The sea should have settled him, but its noise is no help.
I am talking about a man whose doors invite a sail
to cross a kitchen-sill at sunrise, to whom the reek of kelp
drying in the sunlit wind on the chattering shoal
or the veils of a drizzle hazing a narrow cave
are a phantom passion; who hears in the feathering lances
of grass a soundless siege, who, when a bird skips a wave,
feels an arrow shoot from his heart and his wrist dances.
He sees the full moon in daylight, the sky's waning rose,
the grey wind, his nurse trawling her shawl of white lace;
whose wounds were sprinkled with salt but who turns over their
     horrors
with each crinkling carapace. I am talking about small odysseys
that, with the rhythm of a galley, launch his waking house
in the thinning indigo hour, as he mutters thanks over
the answer of a freckled, forgiving back in creased linen,
its salt neck and damp hair, and, rising from cover,
to the soundless pad of a leopard or a mewing kitten,
unscrews the coffee-jar and measures two and a half spoons,
and pauses, paralysed by a sail crossing blue windows,
then dresses in the half-dark, dawn-drawn by the full moon's
magnet, until her light-heaving back is a widow's.
She drags the tides and she hauls the heart by hawsers
stronger than any devotion, and she creates monsters
that have pulled god-settled heroes from their houses
and shawled women watching the fading of the stars.

31 / ITALIAN ECLOGUES

[for Joseph Brodsky]

i

On the bright road to Rome, beyond Mantua,
there were reeds of rice, and I heard, in the wind's elation,
the brown dogs of Latin panting alongside the car,
their shadows sliding on the verge in smooth translation,
past fields fenced by poplars, stone farms in character,
nouns from a schoolboy's text, Virgilian, Horatian,
phrases from Ovid passing in a green blur,
heading towards perspectives of noseless busts,
open-mouthed ruins, and roofless corridors
of Caesars whose second mantle is now the dust's,
and this voice that rustles out of the reeds is yours.
To every line there is a time and a season.
You refreshed forms and stanzas; these cropped fields are
your stubble grating my cheeks with departure,
grey irises, your corn-wisps of hair blowing away.
Say you haven't vanished, you're still in Italy.
Yeah. Very still. God. Still as the turning fields
of Lombardy, still as the white wastes of that prison
like pages erased by a regime. Though his landscape heals
the exile you shared with Naso, poetry is still treason
because it is truth. Your poplars spin in the sun.

ii

Whir of a pigeon's wings outside a wooden window,
the flutter of a fresh soul discarding the exhausted heart.
Sun touches the bell-towers. Clangour of the *cinquecento*,
at wave-slapped landings vaporettos warp and depart
leaving the traveller's shadow on the swaying stage
who looks at the glints of water that his ferry makes
like a comb through blond hair that plaits after its passage,
or book covers enclosing the foam of their final page,
or whatever the whiteness that blinds me with its flakes
erasing pines and conifers. Joseph, why am I writing this
when you cannot read it? The windows of a book spine open
on a courtyard where every cupola is a practice
for your soul encircling the coined water of Venice
like a slate pigeon and the light hurts like rain.
Sunday. The bells of the campaniles' deranged tolling
for you who felt this stone-laced city healed our sins,
like the lion whose iron paw keeps our orb from rolling
under guardian wings. Craft with the necks of violins
and girls with the necks of gondolas were your province.
How ordained, on your birthday, to talk of you to Venice.
These days, in bookstores I drift towards Biography,
my hand gliding over names with a pigeon's opening claws.
The cupolas enclose their parentheses over the sea
beyond the lagoon. Off the ferry, your shade turns the corners
of a book and stands at the end of perspective, waiting for me.

iii

In this landscape of vines and hills you carried a theme
that travels across your raked stanzas, sweating the grapes
and blurring their provinces: the slow northern anthem
of fog, the country without borders, clouds whose shapes
change angrily when we begin to associate them
with substantial echoes, holes where eternity gapes
in a small blue door. All solid things await them,
the tree into kindling, the kindling to hearth-smoke,
the dove in the echo of its flight, the rhyme its echo,
the horizon's hyphen that fades, the twigs' handiwork
on a blank page and what smothers their cyrillics: snow,
the white field that a raven crosses with its black caw,
they are a distant geography, and not only now,
you were always in them, the fog whose pliant paw
obscures the globe; you were always happier
with the cold and uncertain edges, not blinding sunlight
on water, in this ferry sidling up to the pier
when a traveller puts out the last spark of a cigarette
under his heel, and whose loved face will disappear
into a coin that the fog's fingers rub together.

iv

The foam out on the sparkling strait muttering Montale
in grey salt, a slate sea, and beyond it flecked lilac
and indigo hills, then the sight of cactus in Italy
and palms, names glittering on the edge of the Tyrrhenian.
Your echo comes between the rocks, chuckling in fissures
when the high surf vanishes and is never seen again!
These lines flung for sprats or a catch of rainbow fishes,
the scarlet snapper, parrot fish, argentine mullet,
and the universal rank smell of poetry, cobalt sea,
and self-surprised palms at the airport; I smell it,
weeds like hair swaying in water, mica in Sicily,
a smell older and fresher than the Norman cathedrals
or restored aqueducts, the raw hands of fishermen
their anchor of dialect, and phrases drying on walls
based in moss. These are its origins, verse, they remain
with the repeated lines of waves and their crests, oars
and scansion, flocks and one horizon, boats with keels
wedged into sand, your own island or Quasimodo's
or Montale's lines wriggling like a basket of eels.
I am going down to the shallow edge to begin again,
Joseph, with a first line, with an old net, the same expedition.
I will study the opening horizon, the scansion's strokes of the rain,
to dissolve in a fiction greater than our lives, the sea, the sun.

v

My colonnade of cedars between whose arches the ocean
drones the pages of its missal, each trunk a letter
embroidered like a breviary with fruits and vines,
down which I continue to hear an echoing architecture
of stanzas with St. Petersburg's profile, the lines
of an amplified cantor, his tonsured devotion.
Prose is the squire of conduct, poetry the knight
who leans into the flaming dragon with a pen's lance,
is almost unhorsed like a picador, but tilts straight
in the saddle. Crouched over paper with the same stance,
a cloud in its conduct repeats your hair-thinning shape.
A conduct whose metre and poise were modelled on Wystan's,
a poetry whose profile was Roman and open, the bust
of a minor Caesar preferring a province of distance
to the roar of arenas, a duty obscured by dust.
I am lifted above the surf's missal, the columned cedars,
to look down on my digit of sorrow, your stone, I have drifted
over books of cemeteries to the Atlantic, whose shores
shrivel, I am an eagle bearing you towards Russia,
holding in my claws the acorn of your heart that restores
you past the Black Sea of Publius Naso
to the roots of a beech tree; I am lifted with grief and praise, so
that your speck widens with elation, a dot that soars.

vi

Now evening after evening after evening,
August will rustle from the conifers, an orange light
will seep through the stones of the causeway, shadows
lie parallel as oars across the long hull of asphalt,
the heads of burnished horses shake in parched meadows
and prose hesitates on the verge of metre. The vault
increases, its ceiling crossed by bats or swallows,
the heart climbs lilac hills in the light's declension,
and grace dims the eyes of a man nearing his own house.
The trees close their doors, and the surf demands attention.
Evening is an engraving, a silhouette's medallion
darkens loved ones in their profile, like yours,
whose poetry transforms reader into poet. The lion
of the headland darkens like St. Mark's, metaphors
breed and flit in the cave of the mind, and one hears
in the waves' incantation and the August conifers,
and reads the ornate cyrillics of gesturing fronds
as the silent council of cumuli begins convening
over an Atlantic whose light is as calm as a pond's,
and lamps bud like fruit in the village, above roofs, and the hive
of constellations appears, evening after evening,
your voice, through the dark reeds of lines that shine with life.

She returns to her role as a seagull. The wind
flaps the shredded wings of the open-air theatre
which a different role, in life, made her leave behind.
The lake shines with vanished voices. Nina, years later,
who was a small white body trembling for balance,
has calmed her fright, when one of her first tasks
was learning to control the small storm of her hands.
She wrings your heart like a gull's neck when she asks:
"Remember how it was, Kostia?" Yes. Like this cottage
on a wet day with its salt-rusted bolts, its plants
trying to peer through the windows, its black cortege,
some with umbrella petals of funeral ants
for the child, cyrillics on the thin, translucent page
that she once held to the light; remembered lines
like the shallows, the laughable speech she learns
with joy in their future. The stage with its buried sound
of the lake's polite applause. A seagull returns
like a tilted, balancing N for something it remembers.
She remembers the laughter as his demon burns
behind the wings with its eyes like growing embers,
meaning the evil to come. Perhaps the hills were greener
then, and the trees turned excited pages. Remember, Kostia?
Wind rattles the cottage door and his hands open
it and he stares at her, unchanging, and whispers, "Nina?"
as a flock of white papers rises from a desk dustier
than the years when she spread her wings wide for his pen.

i

Races, in this rich valley, inevitably took root.
Cocoa-Spanish Santa Cruz, echoing possession and loss.
In their regulated avenues the orchards of grapefruit
hung easy and thick, and towards the season's close,
when baskets would bubble over with the harvest's freight
and the rind of daylight ripened from green to rose,
as you came down the coiled asphalt ridge with its snaking turns,
even in a climate where beauty is ordinary,
the yellow globes in the leaves glowed like Marvell's lanterns;
then shed roofs began, the lost estate, the scarred quarry.
Imagine the scythes of harvesters on the old estate,
lit not only by the golden fruit but by the cocoa's
lamps in their penetrable shade; imagine a Great
House (not that great in scale, without a scrolled gate
or a keeper's lodge, only a verandah with fretwork eaves,
rocking chairs on the verandah) when the evening egret
left off tick-picking cows for the enclosing leaves,
and close the book then, with the natural rhythm
of its wings and our simplified past. They loved the valley,
rooted in it with a differentiated love,
races as varied as the cocoa pods in complexion,
the snow-speckled trunks enduring the affliction
of envy and hatred, a blight that time would remove,
like the sorrow in the rich soil, until eventually
their history dimmed and vanished into fiction.

ii

Let these lines shine like the rain's wires through Santa Cruz
before they leave me, with the mist, with low clouds that edge
the ridges of modest mountains. Once it grew citrus,
and you could see the yellow gleam of fruit from the ridge
after the narrow gorge from the Paramín side; the Paramín
slopes, which deserve their own rain-lit lines, and driving
through orderly orchards with the kind season coming,
the drizzle tightened into *cuatro* strings, parang giving
joy to the Nativity; then, after His coming, months
of the orange and vermilion choir of immortelles to shower
praise on the Shepherdess, over the unseen (but it runs)
river behind the squat chapel of La Divina Pastora.
One night, coming through the valley in a thick mist
writhing from the headlights, the taxi-driver peers:
"So much o' fog, and it making so cold, dem scientist
predict no surprise if it snow in the next fifty years."
Perhaps it is the fog that erases the sins
of history, that no longer looks or sounds foreign
in the mouth of the valley, despite the visible echo
of Spanish and French in roads in bright gusts of rain,
and, when the rain passes, a shining language. Bamboos grow
over the shallow brown rivulet; they have always bowed,
tossing like horses' heads at the sound, Santa Cruz,
and my peace in the place for whatever time is allowed.

iii

[*for Charles Applewhaite*]

The junction. Divina Pastora. Napkin clouds over Jean's
Hot Roti Shop: a grill with an iron table, a round
of rain from the bamboos like idling engines,
the shadows on Saturday gaining more and more ground
as the week loosens its grip. Sabbath. Now silence
takes root on the roadside like weeds and runs
through Santa Cruz under a bridge, through wild canes,
emptying the brilliant fruit stalls that are San Juan's,
the highway sheds on the verge under indigo mountains
flashing from the far abbey of the Benedictines
like a piece of Cordoba. Into the blue disappears
every Indian vendor with her open-mouthed baskets: tangerines,
eggplant, bodi, and the echo of the name Aranguez,
and the role, Don Gonzalo, in the play's final scenes
in that stone-dusted chapel where you stride up the aisle
with your gravedigger's cough, like a crested palm, to grip
the Joker's wrist and drag him to Hell with a smile
like a crack in concrete. A pillar of the Theatre Workshop
has fallen, and the road is as quiet as your voice,
cherishing your courtesy, Charles, bowing like grass,
drawing its haze over Santa Cruz, across Chaguanas,
lifting a flock of egrets from the cabbage gardens
on the highway to the airport, prayers without noise,
into the myth of a heaven that gradually pardons.

iv

Stand on the star-riddled lawn, then, its iron wet,
slip the gate's latch, the dogs nuzzling your hands,
and feel the dark forest defining its grey silhouette
and familial shapes assemble themselves for distance;
as low-lying mist releases a whiter egret
and the cocoa-pods switch off their lamps near San Juan's
brightening walls. Here begins the lengthening regret
of shadows on the highway as an Asia of saffron cloud
enlightens Aranguez and the calm canes of Chaguanas,
prints the shadows of leaves on whitewashed St. Helena,
sharpens chalk minarets, and reddens a temple's banners.
For a while absence is worth this delight, and then a
difference begins, a map takes shape with its names,
the light looks different streaking the gas stations,
and streets that are waking, St. Ann's, Woodbrook, St. James,
will lead a different life, the imagination's.
Memory will mimic their motions now, Lizzie's and Anna's,
as their children will; what a cloud claims and disclaims
in its closing embrace, gusting past the plane window,
a map whose contours acquire the grid of these lines
across the white page, with two jutting ochre capes,
the fine froth under their mountains, Blanchisseuse, Toco,
then the blue widening to reveal more islands
hidden under small clouds whose shadows predict their shapes.

At the end of this line there is an opening door
that gives on a blue balcony where a gull will settle
with hooked fingers, then, like an image leaving an idea,
beat in slow scansion across the hammered metal
of the afternoon sea, a sheet that my right hand steers—
a small sail making for Martinique or Sicily.
In the lilac-flecked distance, the same headlands rust
with flecks of houses blown from the spume of the trough,
and the echo of a gull where a gull's shadow raced
between sunlit seas. No cry is exultant enough
for my thanks, for my heart that flings open its hinges
and slants my ribs with light. At the end, a shadow
slower than a gull's over water lengthens, by inches,
and covers the lawn. There is the same high ardour
of rhetorical sunsets in Sicily as over Martinique,
and the same horizon underlines their bright absence,
the long-loved shining there who, perhaps, do not speak
from unutterable delight, since speech is for mortals,
since at the end of each sentence there is a grave
or the sky's blue door or, once, the widening portals
of our disenfranchised sublime. The one light we have
still shines on a spire or a conch-shell as it falls
and folds this page over with a whitening wave.

Never plotted, never provided with their proper metre:
the fictions in the dark, on the back shelves of the brain.
"They were riding into the clouds . . ." It doesn't matter
where. No. That is what places it. The rhyme: Spain.
"They were riding into a white page now swept by an echo
of sawing pines and a spring rattling down the gorges"
that fades into silence. I sacrifice them to the pines
which are permanently interesting. Nothing comes of this.
There was a girl there, another Maria, but the lines
propel narrative, so she's gone. She dims into a prose
that ignores motion, which is plot, and all its designs.
"Light broke through the rain in Vieuxfort and horses
grazed, their hides wet," by breakers that foam from the page.
And I stand at the edge of the unuttered, of metamorphosis,
like a monk tired of prayers or an actor of the stage.
There were clouds in the mountains, and horses that perhaps
existed beyond any fiction about them; there was a spring
and another Maria, and in Vieuxfort continuous whitecaps
that are not fiction, as the Atlantic is not, but nothing
is as fresh as the salt wind that comes off its lines.

In late-afternoon light the tops of the breadfruit leaves
are lemon and the lower leaves a waxen viridian
with the shaped shadows greenish black over the eaves
of the shops and the rust-crusted fences that are Indian
red, sepia, and often orange; but by then the light has
ripened and grass and the sides of the houses and even a
rooster crossing a yard blazes like a satrap; the lighthouse
is already on, and bulbs, and they are saying the novena
in the cathedral and the fishermen consciously become
silhouettes in the postcard sunset: this is when a
powerful smell of baked bread drifts and when the hum
of mosquitoes becomes tangible, when the road-ruts
deepen and faces that I love harder every year turn
towards the dusk and deepen also under the coconuts.
It is indigo now and the sea will continue to burn
until the last plane crosses with its green and red
wing-lights headed north and it is now definitely
night and the stars come where they were ordered
to protract the idea of patterns to infinity
and the sand exhales and there on the edge of the sea
green and red lights droning where stars and fireflies breed.

After the plague, the city-wall caked with flies, the smoke's
    amnesia,
learn, wanderer, to go nowhere like the stones since
your nose and eyes are now your daughter's hand;
go where the repetition of the breakers grows easier
to bear, no father to kill, no citizens to convince,
and no longer force your memory to understand
whether the dead elect their own government
under the jurisdiction of the sea-almonds;
certain provisions of conduct seal them to a silence
none dare break, and one noun made them transparent,
where they live beyond the conjugations of tense
in their own white city. How easily they disown us,
and everything else here that undermines our toil.
Sit on your plinth in the last light of Colonus,
let your knuckled toes root deep in their own soil.
A butterfly quietly alights on a tyrant's knee;
sit among the sea-eaten boulders and
let the night wind sweep the terraces of the sea.
This is the right light, this pewter shine on the water,
not the carnage of clouds, not the expected wonder
of self-igniting truth and oracular rains,
but these shallows as gentle as the voice of your daughter,
while the gods fade like thunder in the rattling mountains.